# How it is made

# Lasers

Text    J R Taylor and P M W French
Design    Eddie Poulton

Contents

ff

*faber and faber* in association with Threshold Books

# What is a laser?

Even before the invention of the laser in 1960 the concept was familiar to readers of science fiction, as a 'death-ray'. Although today this image is still very much with us, lasers have many uses which are rather more 'down-to-earth'. They have become very common and essential tools in factories, work shops, offices and now even in our homes.

In the simplest terms, a laser can be described as a source of light or 'radiant energy'. It has, however, many special properties which make it quite distinct from other light sources such as the sun, a candle, an electric light bulb or a fluorescent tube.

The amount of energy that a laser is able to emit, or 'radiate', depends on the material from which it is made. It is possible to use materials in all the states of matter, i.e. **gas, liquid** or **solid**, and at temperatures varying from as low as minus 100°c to many hundreds of degrees centigrade. As a result, lasers come in all shapes and sizes. They can be smaller than a full stop, or so big that they need literally acres of buildings to house them. In spite of this diversity, they all operate on the same fundamental principle.

The rate at which light sources radiate energy is known as their **power**, and this is measured in **watts** (w), e.g. a 100w electric light bulb. The power coming out of lasers varies over an enormous range. It can be as low as **microwatts** (1/1,000,000 of a watt) or as high as **terawatts** (1,000,000,000,000 watts) depending on the type of laser. Clearly, the choice of laser to be used depends on the amount of energy or power needed and the amount of physical space available. For some applications, such as cutting steel plates or welding together sheets of metal, very powerful lasers are required which can be quite large. These lasers, on the other hand, would not be at all suitable for performing delicate operations in eye surgery or for 'reading' a laser disc in a video machine. Most of the telephone links between major cities are now made with optical fibres using lasers smaller than a pinhead as the source of the signals transmitting the information. These lasers would not be at all effective for welding.

In the twenty-six years since lasers have been invented, they have helped to bring about dramatic advances in science and technology. Because the properties of lasers can be very precisely controlled, they can be used to make

measurements with an accuracy not possible using other light sources. They have hundreds of uses in research as well as in industry, and even in our everyday lives, yet relatively few people have a clear idea of what they are or how they work.

To have an initial insight into the operation of a laser, it is not necessary to look any further than the name. **Laser** stands for Light Amplification by Stimulated Emission of Radiation. Amplification is simply the name given to a process in which the 'intensity', or the amount, of something is increased. Most people are familiar with sound amplification in a megaphone or a hi-fi system. In a laser it is light – or rather a special form of light – which is amplified. To understand how this happens we must first understand the nature of light.

Both are lasers but differ remarkably in size. The semiconductor diode laser is the speck on the forefinger of the hand (left) while below are the output beam ports and target chamber of the Lawrence Livermore Laboratory 'Nova Laser System'.

# The nature of light

'Light' to most people means daylight or the light from a candle or an electric light bulb, which enables us to see the world around us. This is known as **white light** because it does not appear to have any predominant colour. In 1665 Sir Isaac Newton showed that if ordinary white light was passed through a glass prism, it split up into the different colours of the rainbow. This process is known as **dispersion** and the range of different colours is called the **visible spectrum**. It was later shown that there were other non-visible forms of radiation passing through the glass prism, as well as the coloured light. If the region just beyond the red beam was focussed with a lens on to a dark object, the object became hot. This type of invisible radiant energy is known as the **infra-red**.

Visible radiation (which is what we think of as light) and infra-red radiation (which we sometimes think of as 'heat') are both types of **electromagnetic radiation** and these, together with **gamma rays, x-rays, microwaves, radio waves** and **ultra-violet** light (which is what gives you a sun tan) make up a continuous range of radiation. This is called the **electromagnetic spectrum**. All electromagnetic radiations travel through free space at a constant speed of 299792900 metres per second, and although at

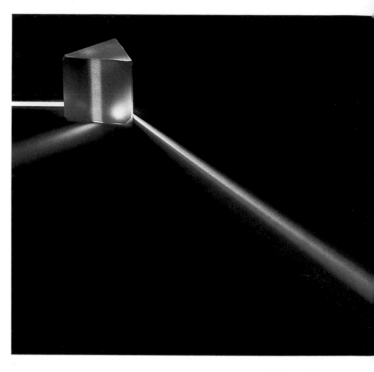

A prism disperses 'white light' into its component colours.

Visible light only represents a small part of the electromagnetic spectrum. Shown below are those spectral regions in which lasers have been demonstrated.

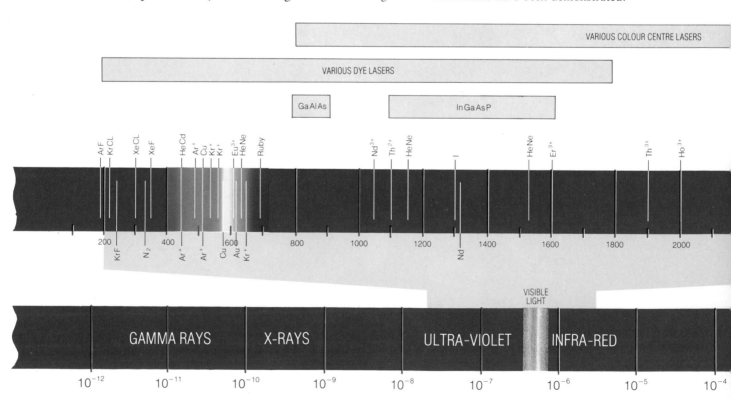

4

first they may seem to be very different, they are all forms of radiant energy with the same basic properties.

How does this radiant energy travel through space? Scientists have two different ways of answering this question. The first is that light travels as a **wave** in a similar manner to water waves. If you throw a stone into a pond it will make circular ripples or waves which travel across the surface of the water. In the same way, light travels as a wave. The distance between two crests or peaks of the wave is called the **wavelength** and the number of waves which go past a fixed point in one second is called the **frequency**. Each different colour of light has a different wavelength. Blue light has a wavelength of approximately 0.0000004 metres or 400 nanometres (one nanometre = 0.000000001 metres), green light has a wavelength of about 500 nanometres, and red light a wavelength of about 600 nanometres. The wavelengths of the electromagnetic spectrum vary continuously from less than $\frac{1}{10}$ nanometre for x-rays to hundreds of metres for radio waves.

The other way of describing light is as a stream of particles. These are called **photons** and each photon of light of the same wavelength contains exactly the same amount of energy. The amount of energy in a photon increases as the wavelength of the light decreases, so a photon of blue light will carry *more energy* than a photon of red light because it has a *shorter wavelength*. This can be understood if you think of the photon as a very small **packet of waves**. The shorter the wavelength of the light wave, the more waves will fit into a packet, so the more energy it will have.

A laser emits light energy in the form of travelling waves, but with a low angular spread compared to ordinary light.

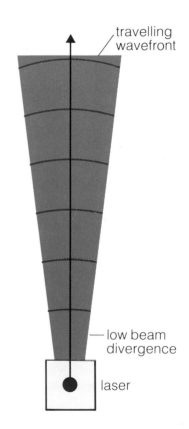

Each colour of light has a different wavelength.

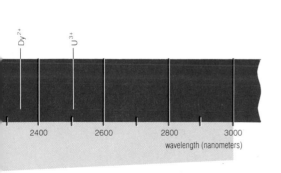

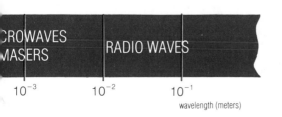

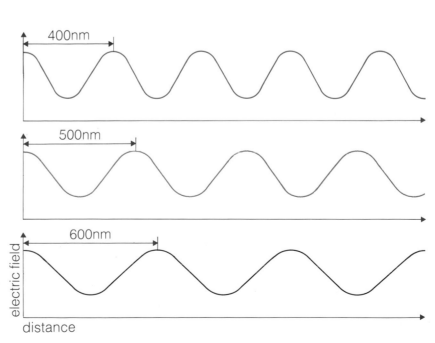

# Absorption and emission of light

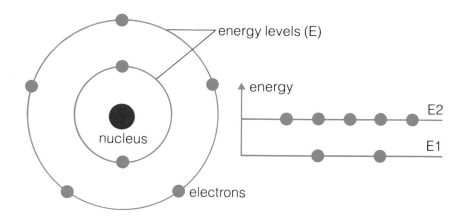

Diagram of a typical atomic structure and the associated energy levels.

In order to explain the way in which a laser works, it is necessary to understand how light is produced and its interaction with matter.

All matter is made up of groups of very small particles. The groups are called **molecules** and the particles are called **atoms**. These atoms themselves are made up of even smaller particles which are arranged in a way that is similar to our solar system. At the centre of the atom there is a **nucleus** which consists of **protons** and **neutrons**. Protons have a positive electric charge and neutrons have no charge. Around the nucleus there are even smaller particles called **electrons**. These have negative electric charge and they travel around the nucleus in much the same way as planets orbit around the sun. The orbits in which the electrons can be found are called **energy levels**. This is because each different electron orbit has a different energy. The further away from the centre, or nucleus, that the electron orbit is, the higher is its energy. The electrons can sometimes go from one energy level (or electron orbit) to another but in order to be in a particular energy level, they must have exactly the right amount of energy. If an electron moves outwards to a higher energy level it must *gain* some energy, and if it moves inwards to a lower energy level it must *lose* energy. The way that an electron can gain or lose energy is for the atom to *absorb* or *emit* a photon of electromagnetic radiation.

We have seen that a photon of light at a particular wavelength has a particular energy. If a photon comes into contact with an atom which has two energy levels with an energy difference exactly equal to the energy of the photon, then an electron in the lower energy level may be moved up into the higher energy level and the photon will be **absorbed**. When this happens the atom is said to be in an **excited state**. It is this process that leads to the colour of most of the things around us. For example, a red dye is one which absorbs all the visible wavelengths except those corresponding to red. Atoms or molecules can only remain in an excited state for a very short time, known as the **excited state lifetime**. This

Albert Einstein, who is best known for his Theory of Relativity, was first to introduce the idea of stimulated emission.

depends on the particular atom or molecule and can be anything from a **millisecond** (0.001 seconds) to a **picosecond** (0.000000000001 seconds). After this time the excited electron drops into a lower energy level (but not necessarily the one that it came from). To do this it has to lose some energy which it does by **emitting** a photon of radiation. The wavelength of this radiation will make the photon energy exactly equal to the difference in the two electron energy levels. When all the electrons are in the lowest energy levels that they can be in, the atom is said to be in its **ground state**.

Another process can also occur which is vital for laser action. This was proposed by Albert Einstein in 1917 and is called **stimulated emission**. If a photon emitted from an atom or molecule comes into contact with another similar atom or molecule which is in an excited state, then the photon can cause, or **stimulate**, another photon *identical to itself* to be emitted. Normally this does not happen, but if there are many atoms in an excited state which are packed close together – as there are in a laser – then it is possible for so much stimulated emission to occur that it becomes more important than normal emission. Using these processes we can now explain how a laser works.

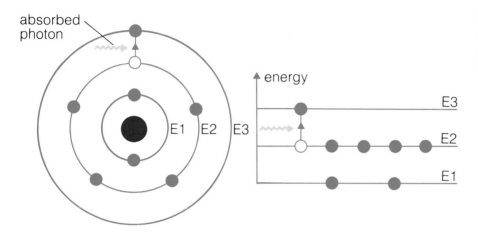

When a photon of the correct energy is absorbed, an electron in the atom gains the energy and moves to a higher orbit.

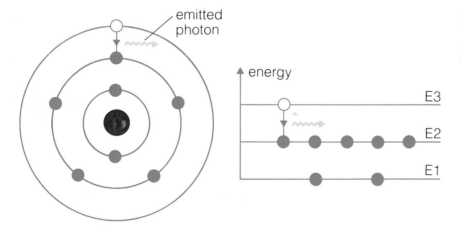

A photon is emitted from an atom when an electron loses energy and drops down from a higher to a lower energy level.

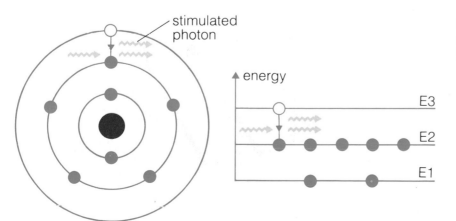

Stimulated emission, a photon causes an atom in an excited state to emit an identical photon.

# How a laser works

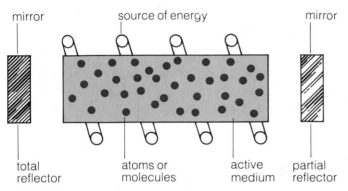

mirror   source of energy   mirror

total
reflector   atoms or
molecules   active
medium   partial
reflector

Outline of a Basic Laser

Any laser basically consists of three items: (1) a material which acts as the light amplifier; (2) a source of energy; (3) and a set of mirrors. The light amplifier is called the **active medium** and can be made out of many different materials which may be solids, liquids or gases. The source of energy is used to **excite** the atoms or molecules in the active medium so that they can produce stimulated emission. The mirrors are used to send the emitted photons back into the active medium so that they can cause more stimulated emissions.

One of the most common sources of energy used in lasers is the **flashlamp**. This is similar to the flashlamp on a camera but much more powerful. When it is switched on it emits light in all directions. Some of this light is absorbed by the atoms or molecules in the active medium and they go to an excited state. In this way the atoms or molecules can **store energy** for a short time (the excited state lifetime) which can be used in the laser. The flashlamp must put the atoms or molecules into an excited state (i.e. store energy) faster than they can **decay** back to the ground-state by normal (or **spontaneous**) emission. This is like having an up and a down escalator between two floors. If the up escalator is faster than the down escalator then the people will tend to get stuck on the upper floor. When a similar process happens with the excited atoms or molecules it is called **population inversion** and this is *always* necessary for laser action.

The excited atoms emit photons of light in all directions. Some of this light will go out through the sides of the active medium, and will be lost, but some of it will go down the length of the active medium, and the photons will meet other

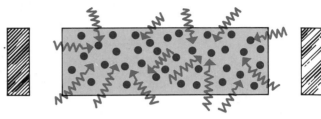

Optical Pumping (blue) excites the laser active medium through absorption.

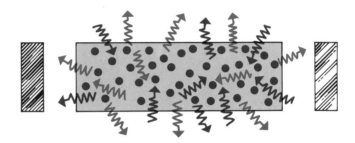

Spontaneous emission (red) occurs in all directions.

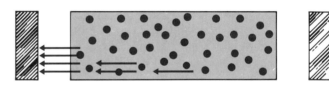

Stimulated emission builds up along the feedback axis of the laser.

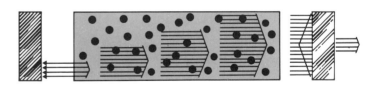

A cascade of stimulated emissions provides amplification and laser action.

atoms in an excited state and produce stimulated emission. The stimulated photons, together with the original photons, will meet further atoms in an excited state and produce more stimulated emission. This process (which is called a **cascade**) continues even after the photons have come out of the active medium because they will bounce off the mirrors and be reflected back in again. In this way just one photon can produce millions and millions of other photons exactly the same as itself by the process of stimulated emission. In most lasers one of the mirrors, which is called a **partial reflector**, will only reflect part of the light that hits it and will allow some of the light to go through. A window pane is a good example of a partial reflector. Most of the light will pass through it, but if you look carefully you can see a weak reflection of yourself. In a laser the partial reflector is made to give a much stronger reflection – often only $\frac{1}{100}$ of the light is allowed to pass through and the rest is reflected. The light that does pass through the laser mirror is called **laser light** or a **laser beam** and because it is made up of photons which are exactly the same, and which are travelling in the same direction, it has many special properties.

Laser light is different from ordinary light in two important respects: it is **monochromatic** and it is **coherent**. Monochromatic means 'one colour' and it is easy to see that if all the photons in a laser beam are the same, they must all be of the same wavelength – and therefore the same colour. This is very different from sunlight which when it arrives at the earth's surface contains all wavelengths from 320 nanometers to 1100 nanometers – all the visible spectrum and

beyond! Electric light bulbs (and the flashlamps which are used to excite lasers) also emit light over a large part of the electromagnetic spectrum. Lasers concentrate all their energy at one wavelength and this can be very useful. To understand how a laser is **coherent** is a little more difficult, and we have to remember that light travels in waves. The photons in a laser beam, because they are produced by stimulated emission, have all their waves exactly in step so that each crest of a wave is lined up with every other crest, and each trough with every other trough. This is described as being **in phase** (or being **coherent**) and if all the waves are added together, the result is a very strong (or **intense**) beam. If we have waves which are not in phase – i.e. waves which are out of step – then when we add them together they tend to average out and produce a much weaker, or less intense, beam. This type of light is called **incoherent**. Finally, if we think about white light, which is made up of many different colours or wavelengths, the waves cannot ever add together **coherently** because all the crests and troughs of the waves cannot ever exactly overlap. In essence, what happens in, for example, a Ruby laser is that ordinary incoherent white light is 'converted' to monochromatic, coherent laser light. We shall see later that coherent light is vital for many applications of lasers.

monochromatic coherent light (in phase) = intense beam

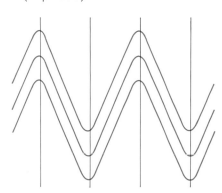

monochromatic incoherent light = less intense beam

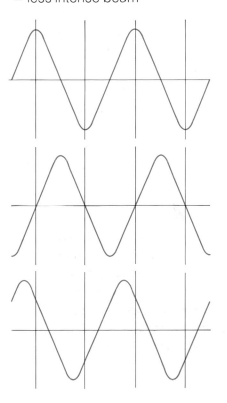

non monochromatic incoherent light = less intense beam

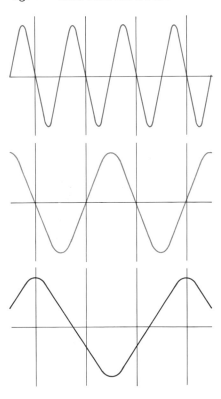

# How lasers are made

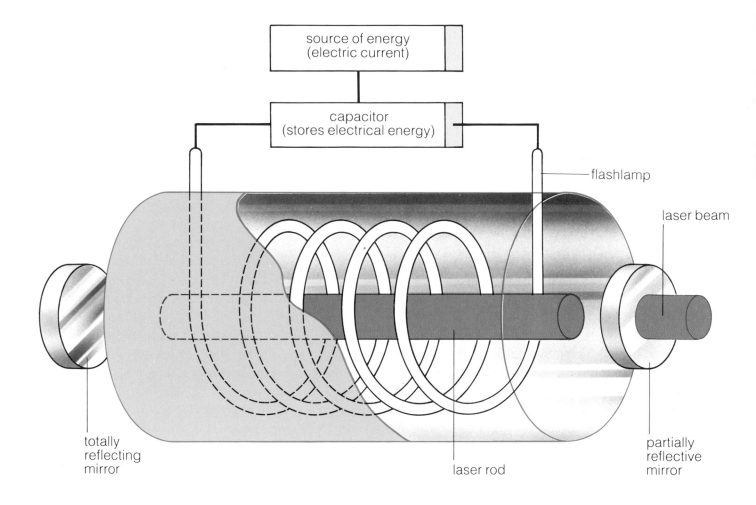

source of energy
(electric current)

capacitor
(stores electrical energy)

flashlamp

laser beam

totally
reflecting
mirror

laser rod

partially
reflective
mirror

Cut-away scheme of a simple pulsed laser system.

There are many different types of laser now available, and the construction of each individual type varies considerably. There are, however, three main processes in the manufacture of any laser system: **electrical**, **optical** and **mechanical**. This section refers to a **Ruby laser**, which was the first type to be invented.

The active medium in a Ruby laser is a long cylindrical **crystal** of ruby called the **laser rod**. The source of energy used to excite the molecules inside the laser rod is a flashlamp. A large **capacitor** is used to drive a very fast burst of electric current through the flashlamp. This causes the gas inside to give out a flash of light, as with a camera flash or a fluorescent light tube. The light then excites the molecules in the ruby rod, ready for stimulated emission.

In the Ruby laser the flashlamp is often **helical** and is wrapped around the laser rod. Around the outside of the flashlamp there is a cylindrical

metal container with a highly polished inside wall which reflects any stray light from the flashlamp into the laser rod. This whole arrangement is sometimes called the **laser head**. Other similar lasers use a slightly different flashlamp which is straight or **linear**. This is usually placed inside an **elliptical** container which has very highly polished inner walls, and which also contains the laser rod. Using this type of container, all the light from the flashlamp is automatically reflected into the laser rod.

The mirrors in the laser are made with great care. The material used to produce mirrors of very high reflectivity must be evaporated in a **vacuum** and deposited on top of polished glass discs in very thin layers that may be less than 0.00002 centimetres thick. The glass discs, which are called **substrates**, are so flat that they have no dips or bumps greater than 0.000005 centimetres deep – and the same is true for the

10

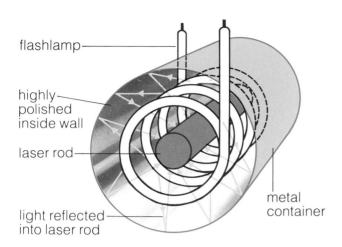

helical flashlamp pumping chamber

flashlamp

highly polished inside wall

laser rod

light reflected into laser rod

metal container

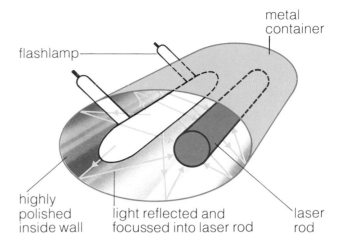

elliptical flashlamp pumping chamber

metal container

flashlamp

highly polished inside wall

light reflected and focussed into laser rod

laser rod

ends of the laser rod, which are also polished. All the optical processes – e.g. producing the crystals for the laser rods, making the mirrors, and polishing the ends of the laser rods and the substrates, must be carried out under ultra-clean conditions. Special rooms are used for these purposes, called **clean rooms**, which do not contain any dust or moisture. It is particularly important to avoid contamination when the laser crystals are being made, since a tiny amount of

impurity can be enough to stop the laser working.

Very precise mechanical holders are needed to keep the mirrors and the laser rod steady enough to reflect the stimulated emission exactly back along the laser rod. If the photons are not reflected back upon themselves, there will be no laser action. In many lasers the positions of the mirror holders must be accurate to within 0.00001 centimetres. It is therefore important to isolate the laser from external vibrations.

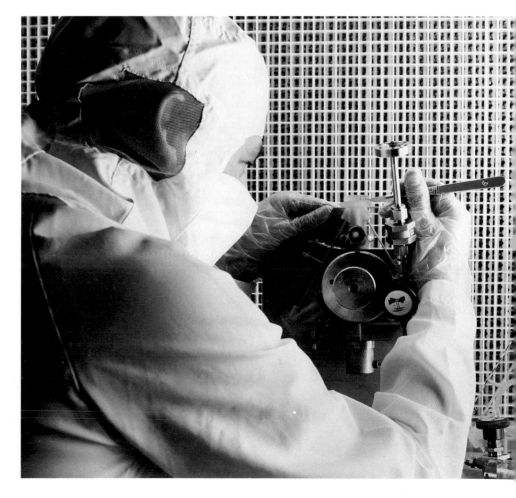

A technician carries out a delicate piece of work in ultra-clean conditions. Note the almost total coverage of the head and body. Even minute specks of dust can effect laser operation- especially with semi-conductor lasers.

# Solid state lasers

The first laser was invented in 1960 by Dr T. Maiman. This was a solid state laser, the active medium being a rod of synthetic **Ruby** crystal. Most solid state lasers have active media consisting of a crystal which has had some of its atoms replaced by atoms of a different element; these are the **active** molecules. In the case of ruby, the crystal consists of a regular structure of **Aluminium Oxide** molecules (the **host** material) in which some of the aluminium atoms have been replaced by chromium atoms. Chromium atoms absorb a wide range of wavelengths in the ultra-violet, green and yellow spectral regions. This is what causes the ruby crystal to be red. The more chromium atoms there are in a ruby crystal, the deeper is the red colour. The original crystal used by Maiman had one chromium atom for every 2000 aluminium atoms, and a laser wavelength of 694.3

nanometres in the red. It is not necessary always to have a crystal as the host material in a solid state laser. Glass and even plastic have also been used. Unlike crystal, the glass or plastic hosts do not have a regular repetitive structure.

The main disadvantage of the original solid state lasers was that their wavelength was fixed. By changing either the concentration of active atoms, or the host material, it was possible to change the laser wavelength of a solid state laser containing particular active atoms – but only by a very small amount. Different wavelengths were obtained by using different active atoms. Some of these are shown in the table opposite, together with their laser wavelengths which are mostly in the infra-red. Very recently, scientists have developed new solid state lasers which can lase over a wide spectral range without having to change the active atoms. For example, Chromium

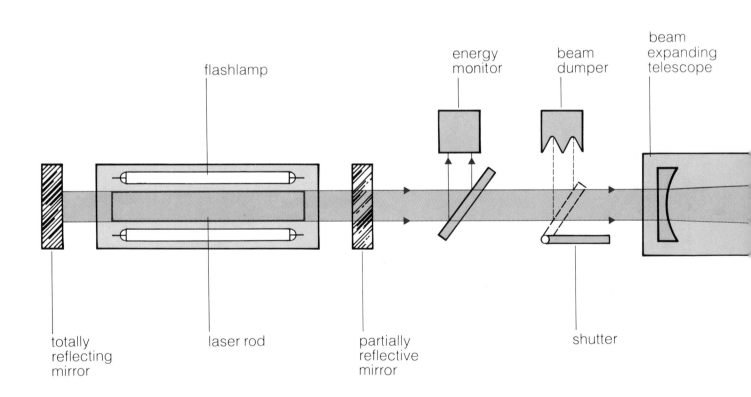

The high power output from a solid state laser can be directed on to the work piece either by reflecting off mirrors in an enclosed flexible arm (as shown here) or through optical fibres.

| ACTIVE ELEMENT | LASER WAVELENGTH |
|---|---|
| Erbium | 1610 nanometres |
| Europium | 610 nanometres |
| Holmium | 2050 nanometres |
| Neodymium | 1060 nanometres |
| Samarium | 710 nanometres |
| Thulium | 1120 nanometres |
| Ytterium | 1020 nanometres |

atoms can lase from 700–815 nanometres in a Berylium Aluminium Oxide host, and Titanium atoms can lase from 660–986 nanometres in an Aluminium Oxide host (Sapphire).

The source of energy for solid state lasers is usually a flashlamp. Mostly the flashlamps are pulsed (i.e. switched on and off in bursts) and this results in a pulsed laser output. The repetition rate can be anything from once every few hours to 5000 times a second, depending on the laser. One of the most common solid state lasers, however, is Neodymium in a Yttrium Aluminium Garnet host or Nd:YAG, and this can be pumped using a continuously operating arc lamp which results in a continuous laser output.

Solid state lasers are most commonly used in high power applications such as welding and cutting, as well as in infra-red vision systems and scientific research.

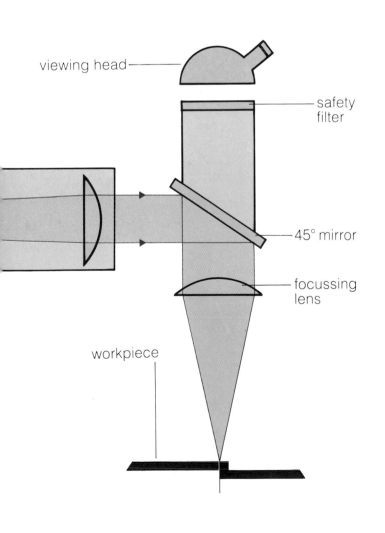

# Gas lasers

Many different types of laser have been built which use a gas, or a mixture of gases, as the active medium. The operational wavelength varies from the ultra-violet to the infra-red depending on the gases used. The table below shows the laser wavelengths of some of the more common gas lasers.

Unlike the solid state systems, the source of energy for laser action in gases is very rarely a flashlamp. Instead, the active atoms are excited by an electric discharge. This is similar to what happens in a neon sign or a fluorescent light tube. An electric current, which is basically a continuous stream of electrons, is passed through a glass tube containing the laser gas. The electrons collide with the gas atoms and transfer some of their energy, thus exciting the atoms ready for stimulated emission. This is called **collisional excitation**. The laser cavity is usually formed by two mirrors, one at each end of the gas tube.

When $CO_2$ (carbon dioxide) is used as the gas, it is possible to build lasers with active laser lengths, or **gain** lengths, as long as 60 m. This very long gain length means that they can produce up to 50 kw (50,000 w) of continuous laser power in the infra-red.

At the other end of the scale, the Helium-Neon laser produces only a few milliwatts (1/1000's w) of power. This works in a slightly different way, because the electrons collide with the Helium atoms and then the excited Helium atoms collide with the Neon atoms to put them into an excited state. Laser action then occurs through

A high power gas laser in a novel arrangement of using a folded beam system instead of a single long laser gain length.

Gas lasers used in the entertainment industry for visual effects.

| LASER | OPERATIONAL WAVELENGTH nm | AVERAGE OUTPUT POWER W | |
|---|---|---|---|
| Argon Fluoride | 193 nm Pulsed | 25 w | ULTRA-VIOLET |
| Krypton Fluoride | 248 nm Pulsed | 50 w | |
| Xenon Chloride | 308 nm Pulsed | 25 w | |
| Nitrogen | 337 nm Pulsed | 5 w | |
| Xenon Fluoride | 351 nm Pulsed | 15 w | |
| Argon ion | 488 nm Continuous | 5 w | VISIBLE LIGHT |
| Copper Vapour | 511 nm Pulsed | 30 w | |
| Argon ion | 514 nm Continuous | 5 w | |
| Copper vapour | 578 nm Pulsed | 30 w | |
| Gold vapour | 628 nm Pulsed | 10 w | |
| Helium Neon | 632.8 nm Continuous | 0.001 w | |
| Krypton ion | 647 nm Continuous | 5 w | |

stimulated emission, in the usual way.

A very useful type of gas laser is the **Noble ion** laser. This uses an inert, or 'noble', gas which is also collisionally excited by an electric discharge. In this case, however, the atoms lose an electron completely and become **ionised**. The most common are **Argon ion** and **Krypton ion** lasers which can generate several watts of continuous power in the ultra-violet, visible and infra-red. These are often used to excite other continuous lasers.

Another important class of gas laser is the **Excimer** laser. In a mixture of gases a burst of electric discharge chemically generates a new molecule, which exists for a very short time (a few nanoseconds, i.e. 0.000,000,001s) and lases during that time. These lasers include Krypton Fluoride, Xenon Fluoride, Argon Fluoride and Xenon Chloride and may produce pulsed powers of up to **gigawatts** (1000,000,000 w). There are many other types of gas or vapour lasers which all work in roughly the same way.

# Dye lasers

An incoming pump laser beam excites a jet stream of dye and allows tunable laser action.

Most people are more familiar with dyes as chemicals used for colouring rather than as laser active media. Their range of colour, however, is what makes them useful to laser physicists, since they absorb light over the visible spectral region. Dyes have the great advantage of being **tunable**, which means that they can change their laser wavelength over a wide range – much more than most other types of laser active media. Not every dye may be used in a dye laser, but there are many hundreds which can, and they lase over the whole spectral region from 250 nanometers in the ultra-violet to 1800 nanometers in the infra-red. Dyes may be used in a laser in the form of a solid (absorbed into a plastic rod), a liquid (in a solution), or a gas (a vapour). They are generally used in alcohol or ethylene glycol (anti-freeze) solutions. In solution, the dye molecules collide with the solvent molecules and transfer energy. This has the effect of making the energy levels in the dye molecules rather vague – or *smeared*. Therefore, when the excited electrons decay back to a lower energy level, they may go to a variety of other energy levels and thus emit a variety of other photons of different wavelengths. Thus it is possible to vary, or 'tune', the laser's wavelength.

The source of energy for a dye laser may be a flashlamp or another laser. In the first case, a linear flashlamp is used in an elliptical chamber through which the laser dye is made to flow. The flashlamps are pulsed so that they can give out enough light to excite the dye molecules. Alternatively, another laser, called a **pump laser**, may be used to excite the dye. This is usually a pulsed nitrogen laser or a continuous Argon ion laser. When a continuous Argon ion laser is used, the dye solution flows very rapidly through a nozzle to give a thin sheet of dye less than 0.02 cm thick. The pump laser beam is focussed down to a spot size of 0.003 cm in the dye jet and some of the dye laser mirrors are curved to focus down the dye laser beam to the same size. This type of laser is capable of producing very short pulses which are used by scientists to investigate very fast processes in nature. Dye lasers are not as energy-efficient as solid state lasers or gas lasers, so they cannot produce such high average output powers. However, their tunability makes them vital for many laser applications.

# Other types of laser

Of the other types of laser, two of the most important are the **semi-conductor laser** or **diode laser** and the **chemical laser**. Though its active medium is a solid, the semi-conductor laser is quite different from the other solid state lasers described earlier. It is probably the smallest laser (as small as 0.1 cm) and the active medium from which the light is emitted may be only microns (0.0001 cm) in size, requiring a microscope to see it. Electricity is the source of energy for this laser, and is applied directly. In construction the semi-conductor laser is similar to a transistor – consisting of a junction between p (for positive) and n (for negative) semi-conductor material. The light is emitted from this junction. Its wavelength and output power depend on the type of semi-conductor materials used. It also depends on the actual structure of the device. A typical diode laser made of GaAlAs (Gallium Aluminium Arsenide) emits 10–20 milliwatts, and is tunable in wavelengths between 750 nm and 900 nm. If many diode lasers are linked together so that their outputs are all in phase, it is possible to generate up to a watt of coherent output power. This arrangement is called a **phase coupled array**. Because of their high efficiency, compact size, and low cost, semi-conductor lasers have become very important in many areas of today's technology.

The chemical laser is also very important. It works by mixing together two compounds which undergo a chemical reaction to form a new compound. This compound is automatically in an excited state (so no external source of energy is needed) and can therefore lase. Hydrogen Fluoride is a good example of a chemical laser. It can emit up to 200 watts c.w. (continuous wave) in the infra-red spectral region. As chemical lasers can be made of considerable size, it is possible to obtain very high laser powers from them.

There are many other types of laser, including the COLOUR CENTRE LASER, the FREE ELECTRON LASER, the ORGANIC VAPOUR LASER and the proposed X-RAY LASER. Basically they all have the same mechanism as the laser action which has already been described.

The Carbon Dioxide gas laser in industrial applications. Above left, a 1200 watt $CO_2$ laser with a robotic arm programmed to weld car doors and above right, a 400 watt system cutting glass screens for miniature televisions.

# High power lasers

There are many applications for very high power lasers, both in industry and in scientific research. These high laser output powers are obtained by either Q-switching or mode locking, and by simply building lasers which are so big that they can store huge amounts of energy that can be released very quickly.

One of the largest and most powerful lasers in the world is the **Nova** system at the Lawrence Livermore Laboratory in the United States. This is an enormous Neodymium glass laser system which emits ten laser beams simultaneously, each consisting of 3 nanosecond pulses containing 10 kilojoules of energy – corresponding to a peak power of 3 million million watts. It cost over $200 million to build and is used to study **fusion**. A tiny glass sphere about 0.1 millimeters in diameter is filled with **Deuterium** and **Tritium** which are special types of hydrogen gas in liquid form. The ten laser beams are focussed symmetrically on to the sphere, producing a shock wave which compresses the liquid to a volume about 10,000 times smaller. When this happens, there is a thermonuclear explosion in which the hydrogen and deuterium fuse (or join together) to form **Helium**. This process is the same as that which takes place in the sun. Scientists hope one day to be able to control it, and to use the enormous amount of energy which it produces, to drive turbines and generate electricity.

The lasers used in industry are obviously much smaller. One of the most common is the **c.w. carbon dioxide laser** which is used for the

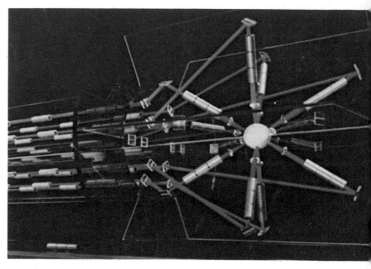

The Nova laser system.

cutting, drilling and welding of metal. When the laser beam is focussed down to a very small spot on the surface of the metal, it is absorbed, and the metal is burnt away, leaving a very clean hole drilled through it. If the spot from the focussed laser beam is moved along the surface of the metal, it can be used to cut out shapes. Welding is also possible if two pieces of metal are placed close together and the focussed beam is moved along the join. The beam melts the edges of the pieces of metal and the molten metal then mixes together, cools down and solidifies as the beam moves on. There are many advantages in using lasers for this type of work because there is no mechanical contact with the metal and so there is nothing to wear out. Also, the laser beam can be easily directed to where it is needed by simply using a set of mirrors.

A fast electro-optical switch is placed in a solid state laser to Q-switch the output.

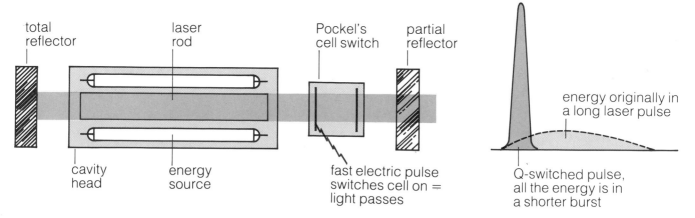

total reflector

laser rod

Pockel's cell switch

partial reflector

cavity head

energy source

fast electric pulse switches cell on = light passes

energy originally in a long laser pulse

Q-switched pulse, all the energy is in a shorter burst

# Short pulses from lasers

The lasers which we have described operate either continuously (eg Argon ion, Nd:YAG, Dye etc) or pulsed (eg Ruby, Nd:Glass, etc). The pulsed systems operate in bursts lasting a few microseconds or nanoseconds and tend to produce higher output powers than c.w. lasers. In general, it is not possible to operate many of the pulsed lasers continuously but it is possible to make the c.w. lasers produce pulses – and this is done for a variety of reasons.

A c.w. laser, or long pulsed laser, can be forced to emit all its stored energy in short pulses and therefore increase its output power (since the same energy is emitted over a shorter time). This is called **Q-switching** and is achieved with the use of a very fast shutter (called a **Pockel's cell**) inside the laser. When the shutter is closed, the photons emitted by spontaneous emission cannot travel backwards and forwards between the mirrors, so they cannot create a cascade of stimulated emission – i.e., there is no laser action. Thus the energy stored in the laser keeps building up until most of the molecules of the active medium are in an excited state. When the shutter is opened, laser action becomes possible, and the sudden cascade of stimulated emission 'sweeps out' all the stored energy very quickly. This results in a powerful pulse of laser light lasting for about 10 nanoseconds. The Q-switching technique is commonly used to increase the output powers from solid state lasers such as Ruby, Nd:YAG or Nd:Glass.

For some applications, such as optical communications, it is more important to have very short pulses rather than high output powers. Very short pulses (less than 0.000,000,000,001 second or one picosecond) are produced using a technique called **mode locking**. This works using even faster shutters inside the laser which may be controlled by fast electrical signals (like in the Pockel's cell), or which may operate automatically.

The second method normally has a solution of dye as the shutter, and is commonly used in solid state lasers. The dye is called a **saturable absorber** and absorbs the photons at the laser wavelength – thus preventing the laser action. After a time, however, so many photons have been absorbed that most of the dye molecules are in an excited state. When this happens the dye solution cannot absorb any more photons and is said to be **saturated**. The cascade of stimulated emission is then free to go ahead – resulting in laser action. This situation lasts as long as the dye molecules remain in the excited state – i.e. as long as the excited state lifetime (see page 7). The dye molecules then decay back to their ground state and are ready for more absorption, so the laser action stops again. Thus the laser operates for short periods of time (i.e. it emits pulses) roughly equal to the excited state lifetime, which may be as short as a few picoseconds. This type of mode locking using a saturable absorber is called **passive mode locking**. A similar process can occur in dye lasers producing pulses as short as 30 femtoseconds (one femtosecond equals 0.000,000,000,000,001 second).

In order to take a photograph of a moving object, a flash is needed which effectively freezes its motion. The time scale of processes in atoms and molecules in nature is of the order of femtoseconds, therefore the mode locked femtosecond pulses can be used to examine the processes taking place by effectively freezing the motion of the molecules.

The output from a mode locked laser consists of a train of very short pulses, each separated by the time it takes light to travel once up and down between the mirrors of the laser.

19

# Optical communications with lasers

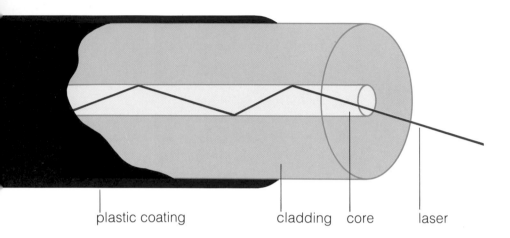

The structure of an optical fibre.

plastic coating    cladding  core  laser

An optical fibre as it is pulled from a molten preform is so fine that it can easily pass through the eye of a needle.

The past ten years have seen dramatic changes in the world of telecommunications, primarily due to rapid advances in the development of semi-conductor laser diodes and low-loss, long-length glass fibres. Telecommunication is the method of sending information over long distances by the use of telephones, telex, telegraph etc. Basically, these devices work by converting text or speech into electrical signals which are transmitted down long lengths of electrical cable to receivers. The receivers then convert the signals back into their original form. The information to be sent is generally **digitised**, or converted into a code which is called **binary**. This code uses only the numbers '1' or '0' which are very easy to convert to an electrical signal, as '1' corresponds to ON and '0' corresonds to OFF. Binary code is written in base 2 so that '5' becomes '101' (i.e. $1 \times 2^0 + 0 \times 2^1 + 1 \times 2^2$). It is easy to see that the faster the electrical signal can switch on and off, the faster the information can be transmitted. A typical telephone system 'switches on and off' at around a few million times a second. It is said to send information at a 'BIT rate' of a few Mega BITs (MBITs) per second. A BIT is simply the smallest amount of information corresponding to one digit of binary (i.e. '1' or '0').

In today's world where people, machines and computers want to 'talk' to each other all the time, it is difficult to send information fast enough. One way to speed up the BIT rate is to use **optical** signals instead of electrical ones. In an optical system, the electrical cable is replaced

by an **optical fibre**, which is made of glass and consists of two concentric cylinders. The thin central section, known as the **core**, has a diameter of only 0.0005 cm, and the outer cylinder, or **cladding**, has a diameter of about 0.01 cm – roughly the thickness of human hair. Around the cladding there is a plastic coating for protection. The glass used for the core is more dispersive than that used for the cladding. Consequently,

any light inside the core is unable to get out – and is guided down the fibre.

The optical signals to be sent down the fibres are generated by very small semi-conductor laser diodes which can produce very short pulses. Each pulse can be used as a BIT of information (i.e. a '1' or an 'ON'). The shorter the pulses are, the more BITs of information can be sent in a given time. A typical optical communication system can send a few hundred MegaBITs per second (i.e. over a hundred times more than a conventional electrical system). Electricity still plays a role in an optical telephone system, as it is necessary to use a microphone to convert the speech into electrical signals which are then digitised and used to drive the semi-conductor laser diode.

The laser diodes emit in the infra-red spectral region where the loss due to absorption in the glass fibres is very low. Sometimes, however, when the information is being sent over very long distances, it is necessary to 'boost' the optical signal. This is done using special laser diodes called **repeaters** every few kilometers which amplify the optical signal as it passes through them.

British Telecom have replaced many conventional copper telephone cables with optical fibre systems. As well as being faster, they are also much cheaper to make. Optical fibre systems are used for linking computers, television monitors and even video telephones. As research progresses, optical systems are replacing many electronic systems, because they are much faster.

A cable ship laying down optical cable inside a protective coating across Loch Fyne in Scotland.

The next generation of supercomputers may well be mostly optical. Some systems do not even require optical fibres. In space, where there is nothing to absorb or block the laser light, satellites can communicate by direct laser beam transmission.

Optical fibre being laid by British Telecom engineers outside Buckingham Palace. The first time an outside broadcast utilized optical fibre transmission was during Prince Andrew's wedding.

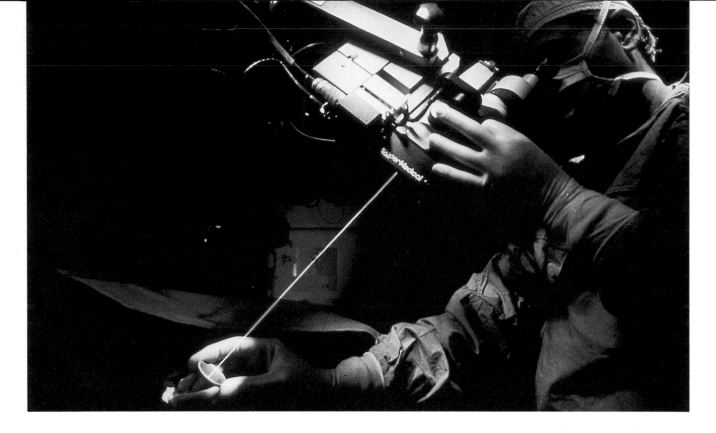

# Lasers in medicine

A surgeon prepares to carry out a delicate operation with a finely focussed laser beam.

As well as high power applications in heavy industry, lasers also find many applications in more delicate areas such as medicine. The high precision with which lasers can be controlled – in terms of their power, wavelength, pulse duration and direction – make them capable of performing very intricate operations. Today, they have become standard equipment in many hospitals.

One of the earliest – and now one of the most common – laser operations is **retinal welding**. The retina is the light-sensitive area at the back of the eye and sometimes it comes away from the eyeball, resulting in discomfort, impaired vision and eventually blindness. Using a beam from a pulsed dye laser, or a Nd:YAG laser, focussed in through the eye, it is possible to weld the retina back into place. Naturally the laser is carefully controlled to prevent any damage and, in fact, the small weld which it does generate does not impair vision at all.

The wavelength-tunable nature of laser light is also useful in surgery, as some wavelengths are selectively absorbed. For example, skin defects – either natural, such as birth marks, or man-made, such as tattoos – absorb light at different wavelengths from normal skin. If a laser, tuned to the right wavelength, is directed on to such a defect, the light is preferentially absorbed by the defect which heats up and vaporizes, leaving a scar tissue. Later it is replaced naturally by

normal skin. Preferential absorption is also used in the treatment of some cancers. There are certain 'marker dyes' which, when injected into the body, get adsorbed by, or linked to, only cancerous cells. By using a laser of the wavelength that is preferentially absorbed by these dyes, the cancerous cells can be vaporised without damaging the surrounding healthy tissue.

Carbon dioxide lasers are used for 'bloodless surgery', replacing the surgeons' scalpel. As the laser beam is passed through flesh, severing blood vessels, it welds the end of the vessels together, so preventing loss of blood. Another promising field of laser surgery is **laser angioplasty**. This uses optical fibres to guide laser light into coronary arteries which have become calcified (i.e. blocked), leading to heart disease and heart attacks. Pulses from an **excimer laser** have been fed down the optical fibres and, in initial tests, have evaporated the calcified material without causing heat damage to surrounding tissue – thus restoring unrestricted blood flow.

In other branches of surgery, lasers are used to shatter and disperse kidney and gall stones. They have been used in brain surgery, where very accurate pin-pointing of tissue to be removed is essential, and they have even been used in cosmetic surgery to remove skin wrinkles in face-lift operations.

# Lasers at war

An infantryman takes aim with a portable range finder on his rifle.

The idea of lasers used as weapons has been around in science fiction for quite a long time. In reality there are many military applications for lasers, both on and off the battle field.

One of the earliest military uses of the laser was as a range-finder. This has now become a simple, portable device which consists of a miniature battery-powered infra-red laser (normally Nd:YAG), an infra-red detector, and a simple, dedicated, microchip computer. It works by sending a short pulse of 'invisible' infra-red laser light at a target and timing the return of the reflected light pulse. The distance to the target (i.e. the range) can then readily be calculated, since the speed of light is a known constant. Modern warfare has also introduced the guided missile or 'smart bomb' which directs itself towards an object using a 'target designator'. This is simply an infra-red laser which is directed on to a target and stays with it. The missile also has a detector, or receiver, which picks up the reflected light from the object, locks on to it, follows it down, and hits the target. Obviously a great deal of research is being done into the kind of devices which can pick up these target designator beams and block them or confuse the sensors on the missile.

The old idea of a death-ray has also become a reality. A massive gas laser has been successfully mounted on a United States Air Force plane and has shot down an air-to-air missile. As laser beams can travel through space without being deflected or absorbed, they have also been proposed for space-based weapons systems which will destroy enemy missiles and satellites. This,

however, will be very difficult to achieve in practice, since the lasers would have to be enormous, and would therefore be difficult to build, maintain, operate and even to launch into space. Also, the actual destructive power of a laser beam is much less than can be achieved with conventional or nuclear warheads.

In order to be able to respond quickly enough to enemy missiles, the 'Star Wars' systems would need very fast, powerful computers (probably optical computers) to control them. So far, these have not been developed.

Similar range finders, thermal imagers and target designators are now standard on U.K. Challenger tanks.

# Holography

Although the concept of holography was introduced by Professor D. Gabor in 1948, it was not until the invention of the laser that holography became a practical technology. A holograph is similar to a photograph, except that a photograph records only the intensity pattern of an image and is therefore two-dimensional whereas a holograph also records the phase information and has the depth of a 3D image. The third dimension (i.e. the depth) arises from light waves which arrive later than the light waves from the front of the image. In order to be able to reproduce a three-dimensional image it is necessary to know about the delay between subsequent light waves (the phase delay).

Ordinary light has random phases (because it is incoherent), so it is difficult to measure any systematic phase delay. Laser light, on the other hand, is coherent. Therefore if one set of waves is delayed in relation to another, it is easy to measure the extent to which they are out of step. A hologram is recorded on a special type of photographic plate (called a **holographic plate**) using a **reference beam**, which comes straight

Holograms – a real object or just an image!

The experimental scheme for recording a hologram.

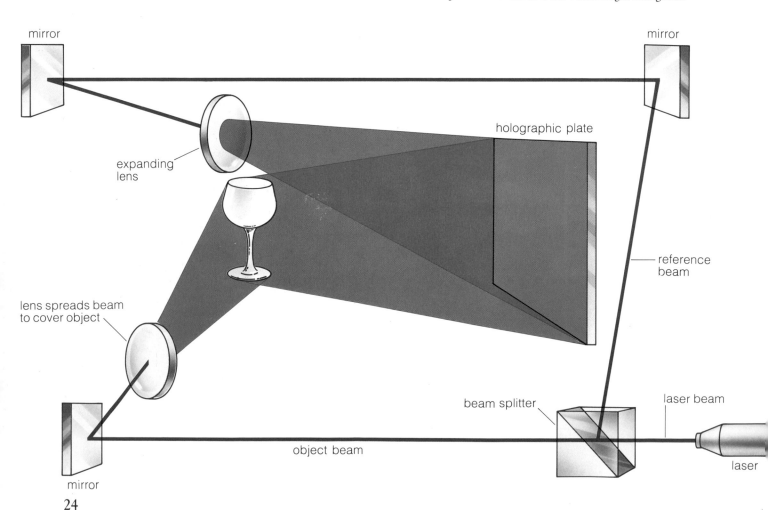

from a laser, and an **object beam**. The object beam has a range of phase delays because it has been reflected off all parts of the object. When these two beams are overlapped on the holographic plate they form an **interference pattern** consisting of light and dark fringes. Where the waves are exactly overlapped, or 'in phase' (i.e. **crest on crest**) there are bright fringes. Where the waves are completely out of phase (i.e. **crest on trough**) there are dark fringes. Hence, by means of a pattern of fringes, the hologram records the phase delay information from all the parts of the object. To reconstruct the object as a three-dimensional image, a laser beam is directed on to the fringe pattern (which makes up the hologram) and the waves in the laser beam are delayed by exactly the right amounts, to form a 3D image. This image or holograph will be the same size as the object. Like the object, it will look different when it is viewed from different angles, whereas a photograph always looks the same from any angle.

There are many applications of holography. As well as being used for displays, exhibitions, decoration and jewellery, they have become very important in the manufacturing industries. One of the most notable applications is **holographic interferometry**. A hologram is made of a perfect specimen of – for example – a propeller. On top of the original another hologram is then made of a propeller of lesser quality. If there is a defect on

Holograms, because they are difficult to forge, are used in the field of security.

the test propeller, when the two holographs are superimposed, the defect (which will have caused further delays in the light waves) will produce an interference pattern. This technique is used anywhere where stress may have caused unacceptable deformations.

To produce holograms, high stability in the recording apparatus is necessary, since very small movements of less than half a wavelength (0.00005 cm) would lead to noticeable phase delays in the reflected light. Because high quality holograms are so difficult to produce, they cannot easily be forged and are used for security purposes – such as on credit cards and cheque cards.

Holograms for popular entertainment and decoration at Light Fantastic Centre of Holography, Piccadilly, London.

# Everyday uses, present and future

Reading a bar code at a supermarket check out.

In the twenty-five years since lasers were invented, their uses have become surprisingly widespread – particularly that of the semi-conductor laser. For example, most modern supermarkets use **bar codes** to label their merchandise. These codes consist of a row of black lines of varying thickness. They are automatically read by a device which feeds the information straight into the cash till, and probably into a computerized stock control system. This device contains a small semi-conductor diode laser, the beam from which is scanned across the bar code. By monitoring the reflected beam, which changes as it goes across the dark lines, the information in the bar code is easily obtained.

Many people now have video or compact disc players in their homes. Lasers are used to read and, in fact, to write the information on the discs. The process is similar to that of an optical telephone system in that the sound (or picture) to be reproduced is recorded using a microphone (or video camera) which converts it to an electric signal. This is then digitised, and the digital electrical signal is used to drive a semi-conductor laser (i.e. switch it 'on' or 'off' according to the binary input signal) which is directed on to a rotating disc. When the laser is on, it etches a 'hole' on the disc, so that the digital signal becomes a series of 'holes' and 'no-holes'. To play back the recording, the disc is again rotated in the

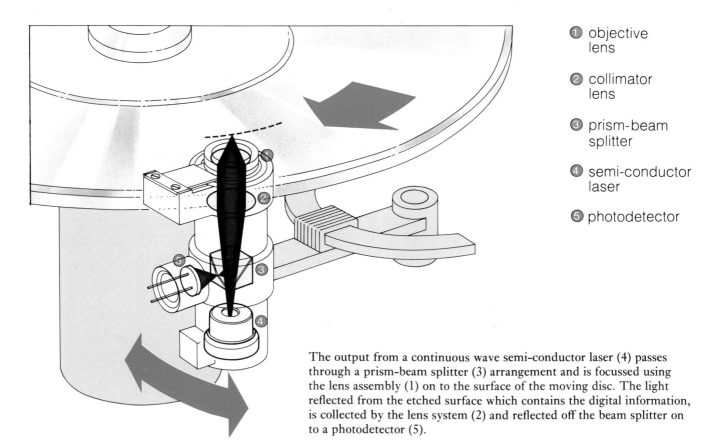

1. objective lens
2. collimator lens
3. prism-beam splitter
4. semi-conductor laser
5. photodetector

The output from a continuous wave semi-conductor laser (4) passes through a prism-beam splitter (3) arrangement and is focussed using the lens assembly (1) on to the surface of the moving disc. The light reflected from the etched surface which contains the digital information, is collected by the lens system (2) and reflected off the beam splitter on to a photodetector (5).

Using a laser land leveller system, it is easy to operate machines at night.

video, or compact disc player. A very small low power infra-red semi-conductor diode laser is directed on to the disc. The reflected beam is then measured by a device which converts light to electricity. As the sequence of etched 'holes' and 'no-holes' moves through the beam, the reflected light changes accordingly. The measuring device thus receives a digital signal which it converts to an electrical signal. This is then transmitted to the speakers (or TV) and reproduces the original sound (or pictures). Using digital techniques it is possible to store more information than on conventional records or tapes, and the quality of the sound or pictures is generally much better. Also, optical systems have the advantage that they do not wear out, as there is no mechanical contact.

Lasers are also used for controlling the motion of machines. For example, on a building site, semi-conductor laser beams are used in conjunction with bulldozers for land levelling. The laser beam is directed along the line to which the land is to be levelled, and a receiver (which detects the laser beam) is placed on the scoop of the bulldozer. All the operator then has to do is to keep the receiver locked on to the laser beam and drive the bulldozer forward. In the building industry lasers are also used for lining up walls, etc. because the beams are always perfectly straight. This also makes them useful for navigation.

There are many other everyday applications of lasers. As well as cutting and welding metal – e.g. in car factories – they are used in clothing factories for cutting out shapes in cloth and then sealing the edges. Increasingly they are being adapted for certain processes in the printing of periodicals and newspapers, such as etching the letters into metal plates. They are also used for laser printing in conjunction with computers and word-processors.

In the future they will become even more important. It has been proposed that they should be fitted in safety devices on motor vehicles, with the laser beam designed to bounce off the vehicle in front and then to control the engine speed so that safe distances are maintained in lines of traffic. As the speed of light is the fastest rate at which information can be sent, computers will become more and more optical as they get faster and are able to store more information. Eventually lasers and optical fibres will almost completely replace electronic circuits. The next step forward in the 'micro-chip revolution' will be with lasers and 'opto-electronics'.

27

# How a laser light show is made

The designer of this book talked to Mark Sutton Vane, the laser artist, at the Laserium in the London Planetarium.

## Q *What is a laser light show?*

A laser light show is a mixture of music and light. The audience listens to music and the artist creates spectacular moving patterns, shapes and areas of beautifully moving colours to the music. These are made by lasers. The Laserium laser light shows started in the London Planetarium in 1977 and have been performed there in the evenings ever since. Each show lasts about an hour. I like to change the shows regularly to keep the latest music in and to add new effects. The Planetarium is a fantastic place for a light show because I can cover the whole of the huge dome with patterns and moving clouds of colour. Also I use the Planetarium's stars and other effects which go well with the lasers.

It is only with lasers, which make such a pure and intense light, that it is possible to produce shows which are really exciting and which have enough different shapes and patterns to be memorable.

## Q *How do you plan it?*

I first decide which type of music to use. Will it be pop, all from the charts, or heavy metal, or what? This sets the theme for the show. Then I start to listen to lots of music, and finally I mix together the sound track. After that I begin to design the laser show. I call this 'choreography' because it is like putting together a ballet. It takes about three months to organise. I have to know all the music by heart so that I can make the shapes move in time to the music.

## Q *How many colours can you use?*

I have two types of laser. One is a 5-watt Argon laser. This makes lots of greeny light. Although its beam is made up of several different shades of greens and blues, I do not separate them, but leave them all in one beam. I then shoot this around the dome to make powerful beams of light which are so bright that they look like glowing wires in the air. The other laser is a one-watt Krypton laser. This is adjusted to make 'white' light. Its beam contains red, yellow, green and blue light, and it makes all these colours simultaneously. The white light is then shone into a prism and dispersed as separate red, yellow, green and blue beams. Each of the four beams then goes on to its own shape-forming system.

## Q *How do you make the shapes?*

Each shape-forming system consists of two tiny mirrors. One of the mirrors can move the beam horizontally and the other vertically. So between the two mirrors the beam can be moved anywhere.

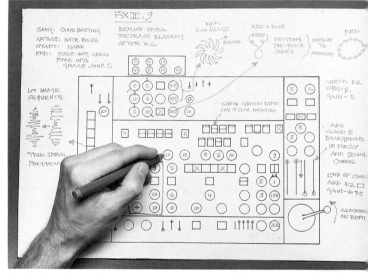

Designing a laser show.

Pattern shapes.

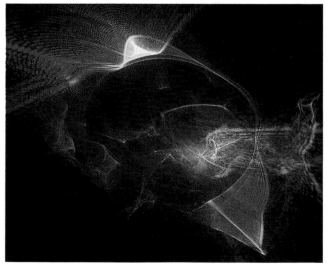

Clouds of colour.

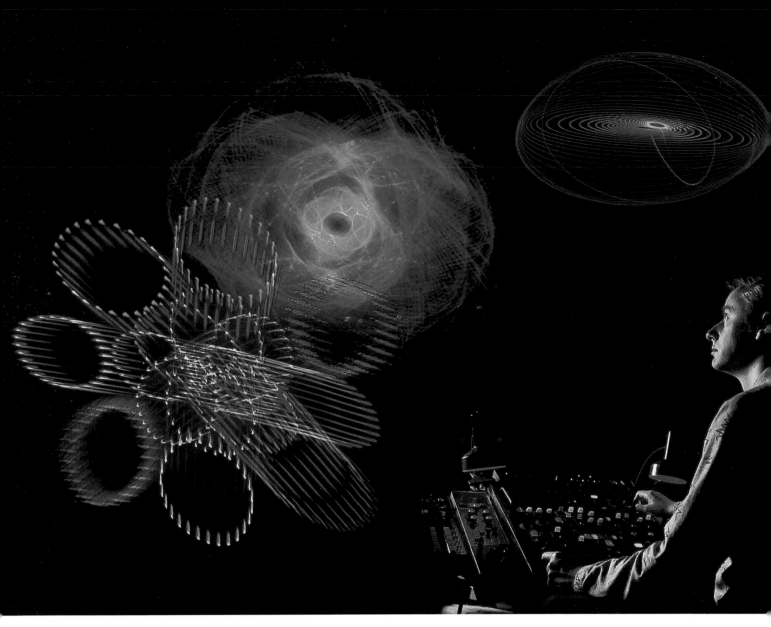

A laser light show performance.

Where the beam hits the white dome it makes a spot of light. If the mirrors move fast enough, the spot goes so fast that the human eye is tricked into thinking that it is seeing a shape – for example a circle – when all that is really there is one spot moving very fast in a circular path. More complicated shapes are made by moving the spot in a more complicated path, but the spot always has to be kept moving fast, tracing out the shape again and again, or else the eye will see just one spot.

Each of the four coloured beams has its own pair of mirrors, so the four different spots can be making four different patterns at the same time.

To make the clouds of colour I take some of the light from the laser, before it reaches the shape-forming mirrors, and shine it through various slowly moving glass discs which have specially moulded surfaces. The surfaces distort and spread out the beams which then make beautiful moving clouds of colour when they hit the dome. You can get an idea of how this works by shining a torch through decorative glass ashtrays or the bottoms of jam jars. For best results do this in a dark room and shine the torch at a white wall. To get different effects, try moving the torch nearer and further from the glass, or move the glass closer and further from the wall.

## Q *Is each performance the same?*

No. I have a large console in front of me when I am performing, and it is covered with knobs, switches and dials. These are used to generate the electronic signals which move the mirrors which in turn move the spots of light. I am continually using these controls to make the shapes that appear on the dome. It is like playing a synthesizer, but the result is shapes instead of sounds. Some shapes are drawn first and then stored in a computer. These are mostly pictures of animals, people etc, and to show them I just push a button.

## Q *How did you start?*

All my life I wanted to do light shows. When I was young I always asked for torches for my birthday. Later I did lots of stage lighting, starting with the school theatre. To be a laser artist it is also useful to have some knowledge of computers and electronics.

## Q *Future light shows?*

It seems that holographic images will probably be brought into laser shows somehow, and as computers become more sophisticated I will be able to make more complex shapes. What I am sure of is that the shows will get even more exciting.

# Laser properties and applications

| TABLE OF SOME COMMON LASERS | | | | | | |
|---|---|---|---|---|---|---|
| | LASER | WAVELENGTH | EXCITATION SOURCE | PULSED OR C.W. | POWER | APPLICATIONS |
| SOLID | Ruby | 694.3 nm | Flashlamp | Pulsed | up to 10 G W | Holography, industrial cutting and trimming |
| | Neodymium/Glass | 1064 nm | Flashlamp | Pulsed | up to GW | Research, surface treatment of semi-conductors |
| | Neodymium/YAG | 1064 and 1319 nm | Flashlamp or arc lamp | Pulsed or C.W. | up to T W. 100 W average C.W. | Fusion research, retinal welding, range finder, cutting, engraving |
| | Neodymium/Fibre | 1065-1145 nm | Semi-conductor laser | C.W. | 1 mW | Research in optical communications |
| | Colour Centre (various crystal types) | 800-3000 nm | Flashlamp, ion laser or most commonly C.W. Nd: YAG laser | Pulsed or C.W. | 3 W C.W. | Research, studies of optical fibres |
| | Ga Al As (semi-conductor) | 750-900 nm | Electric current | Pulsed but more commonly C.W. | up to 50 mW | Laser scanners, printers, compact disc players, laser theodolite, range finders |
| | In Ga As P (semiconductor) | 1100-1600 nm | Electric current | | | Optical communications |
| LIQUID | DYE About 1000 different organic dyes act as lasers | 300-1800 nm / 360-1100 nm | Flashlamp, pulsed laser or C.W. ion laser | Pulsed / C.W. | up to 100 MW / 2 W C.W. | Research tool in semi-conductor physics, spectroscopy / Medical retinal welding |
| GAS | Helium Neon He-Ne | 632.8 nm other lines at 543, 594, 1523 and 3391 nm | R.F. discharge (electric current) | C.W. | up to 100 mW | Holography, construction industry, artistic displays |
| | Helium Cadmium He-Cd | 442 nm | R.F. discharge | C.W. | up to 100 mW | Printing, displays, research |
| | Argon ion | 488 and 514 nm plus lines in U.V. and blue | R.F. discharge | C.W. | up to 20 W | Dye laser pumping, laser blood coagulators, scientific research |
| | Krypton ion | 647 nm plus lines in U.V., blue and yellow | R.F. discharge (electric current) | C.W. | up to 10 W | Laser light shows, displays, medical research, colour reproduction, holography |
| | Carbon Dioxide | usually 10600 nm 9000-11000 nm | Pulsed or R.F. discharge | Pulsed or C.W. | 50 KW to 200 W C.W. | Cutting, drilling, welding, range finding, radar, laser surgery, surface etching, research |
| | Nitrogen | 337.1 nm | Electric discharge | Pulsed | up to 1 MW | Scientific research, dye laser excitation |
| | Xenon Chloride | 308 nm | Electric discharge | Pulsed | up to 10 MW | Photolithography, surface treatment, dye laser pumping |
| | Krypton Fluoride | 248 nm | Electric discharge | Pulsed | up to 10 MW | Scientific research, medical laser |

Power = Energy/Time therefore power depends on whether laser is in a long pulse, Q-switched or mode locked

## Important dates

**1917** Einstein (Germany). Proposal of spontaneous emission.

**1947** Gabor (Britain). Discovery of wave front reconstruction, basis of holography.

**1954** Gordon and Townes (USA). Observe stimulated emission with microwaves – a maser.

**1958** Schawlow and Townes (USA). Propose scheme for optical maser – the laser.

**1960** Maiman (USA). Discovery of the Ruby laser.

**1960** Javan, Bennett and Herriott (USA). Discovery of stimulated emission in He-Ne gas laser.

**1961** McClung and Hellwarth (USA). Q-switch Ruby laser.

**1962** Nathan (USA). Stimulated emission from GaAs semi-conductor laser.

**1963** Lempicki and Samelson (USA). First laser action in a liquid.

**1966** Sorokin and Lankard (USA). Discovery of organic dye laser.

**1966** De Maria (USA). Passive mode locking of the Nd laser.

**1972** Ippen and Shank (USA). Passive mode locking of c.w. dye laser.

**1985** Valdmanis, Fork and Gordon (USA). Generation of 27 femtosecond pulses (the shortest pulse ever) from a passively mode locked dye laser.

# Glossary

**Active medium**   The particular material which, when optically, electrically or chemically excited, acts as a light amplifier in a laser.

**Atom**   The smallest part of an element in nature. Originally thought to be fundamental, atoms are now known to consist of electrons, protons and neutrons.

**BIT**   Short for 'BInary digiT'. In communications, or in computer technology, this refers to the basic unit of coded information: i.e. a zero or a one.

**Capacitor**   An electrical component which is used for storing energy in the form of electric charge. (The stored energy can be rapidly discharged through a flashlamp.)

**Cavity**   The optical assembly of a laser, usually consisting of two or more highly reflecting mirrors which feed light back into the active medium of the laser.

**Cavity head**   The mechanical construction placed in the cavity which contains the laser-active medium and, generally, the excitation flashlamp and reflective chamber.

**Coherent**   The term which is used to describe waves which are in step, or in 'phase', so that their crests and troughs overlap in time and space.

**Collisional excitation**   The process by which an atom, molecule or electron in its excited state collides or hits another atom or molecule in its ground state, so that the excited species transfers all its excess energy to the second atom or molecule.

**c.w.**   'Continuous wave'. When applied to lasers this refers to a light output which is constant as long as the excitation is applied to the active medium.

**Digital**   Refers to systems with discrete values. Usually when applied to computers or communication systems only two values of signal are necessary – zero and one. All other numbers or words can be put into a code of digital form.

**Dispersion**   The process by which a beam of light splits up into the different wavelengths, or colours of light, from which it is made.

**E.M. radiation**   'ElectroMagnetic radiation'. Waves made up of a vibrating electric and magnetic field, which are a form of travelling energy. All e.m. waves travel at the same speed through free space; the 'speed of light': $3 \times 10^8$ metres per second. Visible light is only a minute part of the range of e.m. radiation which exists.

**Electron**   One of the elementary particles of physics which are needed to build atoms. Electrons have a negative electric charge.

**Excimer**   An *excited dimer*. This is a system of two similar atoms which, in their excited states, join together and form a molecule in an excited state. Some can be very efficient lasers.

**Excited state**   The description of an atom or molecule when it is in an energy level with more energy than in its normal or 'ground' state.

**Frequency**   The number of vibrations or complete cycles in a unit of time, noted by cycles per second, or Hertz.

**Ground state**   The state which describes an atom or molecule when it is in its lowest energy level.

**Helical flashlamp**   A flashlamp in the shape of a helix, or a corkscrew, which in some lasers is coiled about the laser rod for excitation.

**Interference**   When applied to light, this refers to the overlapping of coherent light-waves, resulting in patterns of light and dark fringes. Bright fringes are generated by constructive interference (where peaks overlap with peaks) and dark fringes by destructive interference (where peaks overlap with troughs).

**Joule**   The unit of all forms of energy. One joule of energy emitted in one second is one watt of power.

**Maser**   This stands for Microwave Amplification by Stimulated Emission of Radiation. Masers were discovered before lasers and they operate in just the same way but with much longer wavelengths (0.2mm to 1mm instead of nanometres or micron waves).

**Mode locking**   The process which generates a very short burst of light, emitted from a laser once on each round-trip of the laser cavity. The pulses generated are therefore spaced at regular intervals.

**Monochromatic**   Relating to radiation which is made up of a very narrow spread in wavelengths (ideally only *one* wavelength).

**Neutrons**   An elementary particle which has no charge and is a basic building block of atoms, found in the nucleus.

**Nucleus**   The central part of the atom, containing nearly all the mass, which is positively charged.

**Optoelectronics**   The technology which covers the introduction of optical phenomena to the field of electronics. Its aim is to make faster circuits through the interaction of optical and electrical effects.

**Partial reflector**   A mirror which allows some light to pass through it, and reflects the remainder.

**Photon**   The quantum, or elementary particle, of electromagnetic radiation.

**Pockel's cell**   An electro-optical instrument designed to rotate the plane in which a light wave is travelling, by applying an electric field or pulse. It can be used inside a laser to Q-switch or mode lock.

**Population inversion**   A condition necessary for laser action. It is produced when, in an atomic or molecular system, the number of atoms or molecules in the excited state is greater than the number in an energy state below. This is usually achieved by rapidly supplying energy to the system.

**Protons**   A basic particle of nature which is positively charged and is found in the nucleus of all atoms.

**Pump laser**   A laser which is used to excite and cause laser action in another laser-active material.

**Q-switch**   The laser process in which the laser is prevented from lasing while the population inversion grows and grows and then is rapidly allowed to operate, so that an enhanced energy is obtained in a very short pulse.

**Spectrum**   Any distribution of a portion of electromagnetic radiation – for example, the visible spectrum, obtained with a prism, or the wavelengths obtained from a laser beam dispersed by a prism.

**Spontaneous emission**   This occurs when atoms or molecules are in their excited states. The excess energy is lost by returning to the ground or a lower state, accompanied by a photon of light whose energy or wavelength is determined by the difference in energy of the two levels.

**Stimulated emission**   Takes place when a population inversion exists in an atomic or molecular assembly, and an incident photon of the same energy as an allowable energy transition causes the emission of an identical photon.

**Substrates**   The material, generally metal or glass, on which laser mirrors are fabricated. These pieces generally have a flatness better than one tenth of the wavelengh of the light to be reflected off them.

**Ultra-violet and vacuum ultra-violet**   Electromagnetic radiation from 10nm to about 400nm. The vacuum ultra-violet (below about 200nm) is absorbed as it passes through air, so it needs to be in a vacuum to be transmitted.

**Vacuum**   A volume in which all, or the major part of, the molecules of the gases which make up air have been removed.

**Visible**   The part of the electromagnetic spectrum between approximately 400nm and 750nm which appears coloured from blue through to red.

**Wavelength**   The distance in a continuous wave train between next nearest peaks or troughs.

**White light**   The term used to describe a form of light – for example, daylight – which contains all the colours of the visible spectrum at such intensities that no colour appears to dominate.

**X rays**   Radiation lying below 10nm. X rays can penetrate, or pass through, materials to a degree depending on the wavelength of the X ray.

# Index

# Acknowledgements

**Illustration credits**
Photographs: Advance Technology Publications Inc 18; Article Number Association (UK) Ltd 26 (top); Barclaycard 25; Barr and Stroud 23 (bottom); British Telecom 20, 21; Coherent 16; Geoffrey Drury 3 (top); Ferranti Industrial Electronics Ltd 11, 14, 17; Light Fantastic Ltd 24, (G Drury) 25; London Features International (S Fowler) 15; Lucasfilm Ltd 2; Lumonics Ltd 13; Mansell Collection 6; Philips Electronics 26 (bottom); Pilkington PE Ltd 23; Eddie Poulton Design (G Drury) 28, 29; Science Photo Library (Lawrence Livermore National Laboratory) 3 (bottom), (D Parker) 3, (A Tsiaras) 22; Spectra-Physics 27; Standard Telephones and Cables PLC 21.

Diagrams and drawings: Dennis Hawkins 5 (below), 8, 9, 10, 11, 18, 19, 20, 24; Eddie Poulton 4, 5 (top), 6, 7, 12.

Picture research: Christine Vincent

First published in 1987
by Faber and Faber Limited,
3 Queen Square, London WC1N 3AU

Typeset by August Filmsetting, Haydock, St Helens

Printed and bound in Italy by New Interlitho, Milan

The How It Is Made series was conceived designed, and produced
by Threshold Books Limited,
661, Fulham Road, London SW6 5PZ

General Editor: Barbara Cooper

British Library Cataloguing in Publication Data

Taylor, J. R.
    Lasers.—(How it is made)
    1. Lasers—Juvenile literature
    I. Title    II. French, P.M.W.    III. Series
    621.36'6    TA1682
    ISBN 0–571–14731–3